A Collection of Poems for 6-9 year olds

FOR M, D AND T

Shhh Please! This is a Library

Squeak, squeak,

Shhh please!

Squeak, creak,

A whisper;

"Over there!"

The smell of polish and old books.

Lost in words

The flip of pages

Knowing glances

The air is thick with thought.

Gentle, peaceful, Heavenly bliss

People absorbed in print.

Where would you go?

If I could go anywhere at all
It would be Devil's Chair at Victoria Falls
With my friends peering over the ledge
A swim in the pool
You can't act the fool
Or with the water you'll be over the edge!

Let's let people 'be'

Pink for girls and blue for boys?
Thank Goodness all that has gone.
If girls like boy-jeans
And boys like skirts
Don't hurt their feelings
'Cos "Ouch!" that hurts

They're only clothes –
Let people be free
To wear what they like
And be who they please.

Letters and Words

Letters and words all over the page
It's not 'til you're older you learn...
That letters have sounds and sounds make words
And words make your story in turn.

Zero Years!

If we are 'one' the year after we're born
And then two and then three and then four,
It's fine with me and so plain to see
That that's counting in years for sure.

So, what I'd like to know, is 'if you're zero
Does that make you nothing at all?'

Scary!

Things the first time can be scary
Like striding a gap on the train,
Keeping still with a wasp right by you
Or walking on ice in the rain.
Asking for help when you're terribly shy,
Stroking a horse that's way up high

There are lots of other things as well
But be strong, and be bold,
So you'll have stories to tell
Later in life - when you're older.

It’s not fair!

It’s not fair
He pulled my hair!
Why did he do that to me?
I won’t do it back
‘Cos I’m better than that;
I’ll play with my friends over there!

Marmite

Shiny, sticky, dark and tricky
How much to put on the knife?
It tastes so strong
If it sticks on your tongue
So best just start with a ‘try’

Stairs

Nine, ten, eleven, twelve…

I count out loud or just in my head

Stairs are a clever invention;

They help with my counting

And they get me to bed!

Outside they're called 'steps'

Inside, 'stairs' you see,

But whatever their name;

The result is the same

And they get me from A to B

Moving stairs or 'escalators';

(You get those in airports and shops)

Hold onto the rail!

As who knows? In the sale

Overloaded

It might suddenly stop!

The News

6 o'clock and then at 10
But I'm usually in bed by then
The news is what's gone on today
Good things, bad things and some okay;
Hospitals, banks and then the weather
I'll watch it so I get to be incredibly clever

Kisses

25 million times 5's a big sum
It's more than I can count on my fingers and thumbs
Drops of rain on the sea? Or kisses from Mum?
Grains of sand on the beach?

Maybe it's how many stars I can't reach?

Maybe it's the snowflakes that fall when it's colder
Whatever it is
One thing's for sure
I'll work it all out when I'm older!

Please and Thank-you

If somebody does something for you
Say 'thank-you' because it was kind.
If you need something doing, say 'please'
And tell them the thing on your mind.

If you get used to this

It's not a pain in the butt

'Cos you'll say it without even thinking,

No ifs or buts

With your manners you'll strut

And you'll see it's as easy as blinking.

<u>Morning</u>

I don't

Want

To

Get

Up

Today

But

I'll do it

Because

It

Will

Be

Okay.

I was warm in my bed,
My throat's a little sore
But I'll see how I go
Put my feet on the floor

I'm actually okay
And it's a beautiful day
I've brushed my teeth
Meet my friends on the way

I'm glad I got up
I've had some good luck
Which I wouldn't have had if I had stayed!

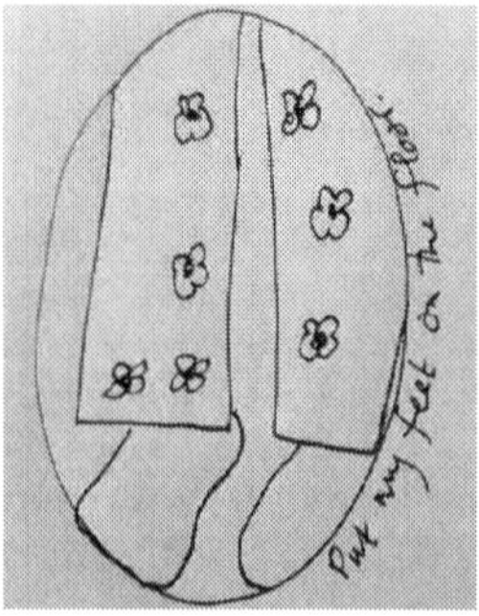

Miss Huff has had enough!

When my teacher says "Class that's enough!"
Her voice sounds terribly gruff
Her patience wears thin
When there's a terrible din
I think we'll be kind to Miss Huff!

Ten more minutes

I hope I can get to the end
My mind is beginning to bend.
I've worked hard all day
My Dad's on his way
From home so it's nearly the end.
Ten more minutes; I'll be off scot-free!
But I'll be back again tomorrow
Bright-eyed, bushy-tailed, you'll see!

Rhymes from Old Times!

Oranges and Lemons said the
Bells of St Clements
What's all that about? Beats me!
There are so many rhymes about
Olden-day times
Ring-a-roses, Scottish Bluebells,
Polly's kettle for tea.
They're from long ago,
From our past
So we know
Where we've come from
So now here we be!

<u>What will I be like?</u>

I don't know if I'll be good at one particular thing,
Or maybe quite good at them all.
I like writing not Maths
And sing songs in the bath
I can plait hair
And love games with a ball.

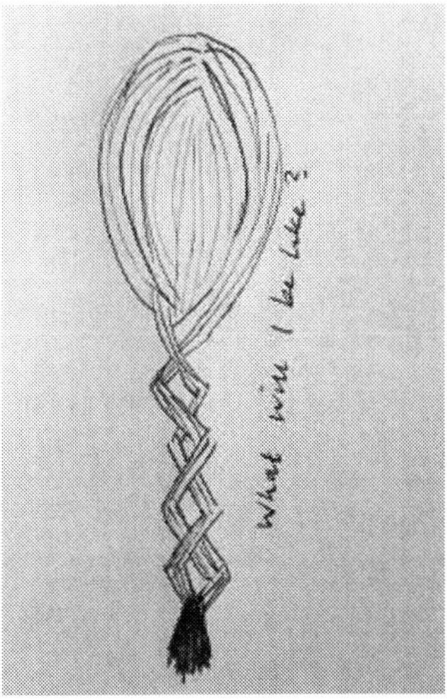

Remembering the Colours of the Rainbow

Richard of York Gave Battle in Vain
Helps you remember the colours by name;
Red Orange Yellow Green Blue Indigo Violet,
Recalling them all?
It's just like a game!

Rainbows are made when there's rain and there's sun
All the colours of light divided,
I never want them to go
They're so pretty you know,
And there's GOLD at the end I've decided!

Medicine that's Yuk!

You need to take your medicine
No matter how horrid it tastes!
Sometimes it tastes like banana
But sometimes it's like eating paste.

If medicine fills you with dread
Then try to do this instead;
Eat it with yoghurt or drink it with juice
Don't waste it, stay calm, sensible head!
'Cos medicine helps you get better
So be a brave thing; hold your nose and then sing,
As it means you can get out of bed!

The Things People say!

If someone says you're to 'take a pew'

It means sit down, have a rest, so do!

If they say 'in a bit'!

They'll see you real soon

And 'laters!' that means the same thing.

If they say 'on your Todd' it

Means on your own,

And if you're 'cool' or you're 'solid' they like you, you know!

So Many names!

Why can't birds just be birds?

There are soooo many types!

Like blackbird, chaffinch and parrot

With cats it's the same

You get so many breeds

Like Siamese, Burmese or Persian

When I grow up I might get a pup
But its breed?
I don't know for certain!

Out for a Spin!

I watch my Mum as we drive along;
Driving looks so easy!
But I know it's not
It must take A LOT
To drive so no-one gets queasy

She does all the gears
Steers us quite straight
Her feet on the pedals
As we squeeze through the gate.

It's a busy time
She never keeps still; checking mirrors, pressing buttons and levers

'Til we scrunch on the drive in front of the house

We drove carefully, I hope you believe us!

TIME

"What time?"

"Quarter to nine?"

If I leave at eight

Will I be late?

A clock with hands and a circle divided

Or a screen with numbers to 24

Time goes by

It will surely fly

Whichever way I look

As I rush out the door

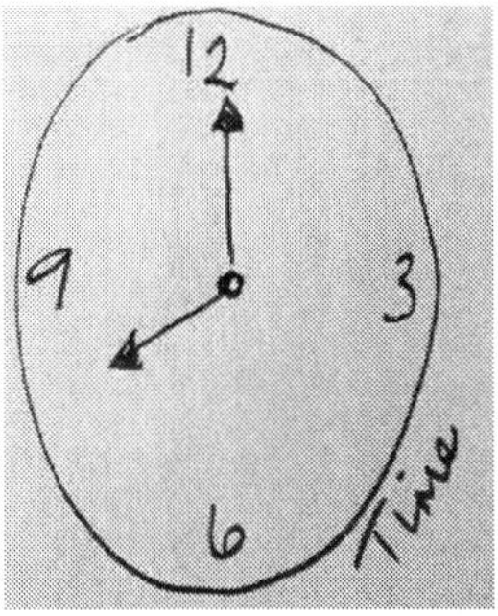

Bits of Everyone

When I started my life
I was given something called genes,
They're bits of my Mum, Dad and Gran
(Everyone who lived before me it seems!)
It's a lottery you see
What you get is how you'll be
Plus where I grew up; that's what's made me Me!

Threading a needle

Twenty-five times I've tried to thread this needle
I've tried over and over again
I'll keep at it you see
'Til it's ready for me
To stitch patterns for presents for friends

Longest Poem

I want to write a poem
That's really, really long
I could write it on some toilet paper
That's really, really, strong

In and out the bedrooms
And out of the front door...
It could stretch along the street,
Over the roundabout, through the woods

Onto the motorway
Merge with all the cars
My poem would keep on going
I'm not really sure how far!

Maybe it would travel abroad
And wrap around the World?
I could get a message to everyone
When the loo-roll had unfurled.

A message through my words to love and not to hate,

A message that started when it left my garden gate.

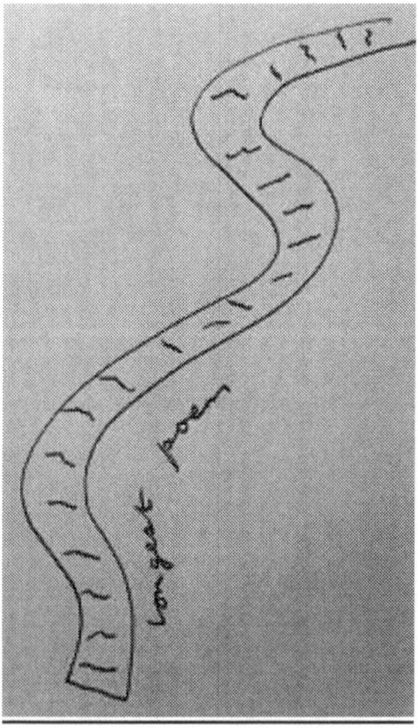

Money doesn't grow on trees!

Money doesn't grow on trees

So I'll just have to save-up

To buy what I please

What grows on trees are berries, fruit and nuts

So I'll have to save-up

With no ifs or buts

In order to buy what I please

You see there aren't pound-notes instead of leaves

So I'll have to save-up

To buy what I please!

When You Get Sad

Losing someone or something,

Or if you're feeling ill,

Animals being badly treated,

Or crimes against your will.

Poor people, the homeless and wars abroad,

Being grounded, told-off

These things and more

Can make you feel sad so try this instead...

Just be your beautiful self

And know good times still lie ahead.

<u>Imagine</u>

What if you were in the Circus?

Maybe a clown - on a bike?

What do you think that that would feel like?

Or a flamingo on one leg

Standing so meek

Do you think you'd fall over?

Reaching behind with your beak?

Or a cloud floating by

Heavy with rain

Leaking on the rooftops

Then disappearing again

So many things to imagine you could be

So much fun for someone dreamy like me!

Bubbles or not?

Sometimes I like bubbles in my bath
Because they sparkle and fill me with glee
Sometimes I want the water just plain
So I can see the big bruise on my knee!

Twenty-four hours

Twenty-four hours equals one day
Hours can pass quickly or go very slow.
Depends what you're doing it strikes me,
As to how the hours will go!
They drag along slowly if something fills you with dread
(If it bores you and you'd rather be elsewhere instead)

If it's fun they pass quickly
'Cos you don't even know
So enjoy what you do
And the time quickly will go!

How do I feel?

Happy, sad, frustrated,

Embarrassed, shy, elated,

Bored, excited, proud,

Boisterous, chilled or loud.

It's important how I deal with my feelings

It can make my friends laugh or else cry

So get my meaning, take care of your feelings

If you can't, you really must try!

Goodbye

Cheers, So-long, laters, goodbye

So many words when we go.

In a bizzle, see you soon, farewell and I’m gone,

With a smile or a tear in your eye?

21961059R00020

Printed in Poland
by Amazon Fulfillment
Poland Sp. z o.o., Wrocław